Jacqueline Igosa

4/16/23

ISBN: 979-8-9877712-1-1 (Paperback)
ISBN: 979-8-9877712-0-4 (Hardcover)
ISBN: 979-8-9877712-2-8 (Ebook)

Library of Congress Registration number: TXU002356779

Any references to historical events, real people, or real places are used fictitiously. Names, characters, and places are products of the author's imagination.

Illustration by Jackie Agossa.
Book design by Jackie Agossa.

First printing edition 2023.

Www.mymindismagic.com

Acknowledgement

As I got older I realized the power of my words. To all the children in the world, dream big. Never let anyone tell you, you can't dream big. Turn your dreams into reality just like Layla.

Thank you to everyone who has Pre-ordered / Ordered My Mind Is Magic.
Thank you to all my readers. Thank you to the Parents/ Guardians who bought my first book.
A special Thank you to my friends and family.

Thank you to Chelsea for being there every step of the way. She stayed up with me every night and motivated me to keep going.
Thank you to Yamilet for helping me edit my children's book.
Thank you to Zeyana who was my first little reader.
Thank you to Don for ordering my first book.
Thank you to Melody for helping me bring my turtle illustration to life.
Thank you to Barbra for helping me through the self-publishing journey.

MY MIND IS MAGIC

WRITTEN AND ILLUSTRATED BY

JACKIE AGOSSA

Layla loves turtles. She loves their pretty shells and the little turtle tanks that they live in. Layla did not know anything about turtles and she did not have any money. Would she ever have her own turtle? Layla wasn't so sure. She sat in the kitchen and imagined what her turtle would look like and what she would name him. Layla's mom and dad knew that Layla wanted a turtle more than anything.

Layla's mom and dad always told her she could use her mind to get anything she imagined. Layla asked her mom to show her how. Later that day, Layla's mom took her to a car shop and pointed to a car she really wanted. It was a beautiful pink car.

As they drove home, Layla was very confused about what the car had to do with using her mind to get what she wanted.

At night, Layla went to her parent's room, with lots of questions. How am I going to get what I want if you can't get the car that you want, she asked.

Laylas mom said, "sweetie, things take time. I will get the car one day." I already imagined myself driving it. Not only that, but I have money saved and I will work really hard at my job to save more money to buy it. This is called manifestation. It means whatever you focus on or imagine will come to you.

This is the important part, Layla because it can be good or bad. That is why I always tell you to focus on the good things rather than the bad things. Then Layla asked, why didn't you get the car you wanted? Great question, said Layla's mom, I want you to understand that sometimes things don't come out as planned.

Sometimes you can really want something and it's not the right time so it doesn't happen when you want it to happen, but just remember if it's meant for you, it will happen when the time is right. Always remember that your mind is magic, Layla."

Layla, do you want to know what I am manifesting? Asked Layla's dad. Yes, said Layla enthusiastically. I want to go on a family vacation. As your mom said I have to plan for it and save money to get what I want.

The first step is knowing the goal. The second step is to create a plan. The third step is to work on the goal. The fourth is to stay focused. The fifth step is to stay positive.

As Layla's mom walked her into her room she asked, "Layla, what is one thing you really want? With excitement she said, I want a turtle mom! A turtle? Layla's mom kissed her on her forehead and asked "what steps are you going to take to get your turtle?"

Stay positive

Stay focused

Work on your goal

Create a plan

Know your goal

Chores list
• Laundry
• Dust
• Mop
• Sweep
• Garbage

The first step is knowing my goal. The second step is to create my plan. The third step is to work on my goal. The fourth is to stay focused. The fifth step is to stay positive. That's what I love to hear said mom.

The next morning, Layla woke up excited and asked her mom to take her to the pet store. They quickly got ready and drove to the pet store.

Layla tugged on the store owner's shirt and asked politely "can you take me to the turtles." As they walked over to the turtles, Layla asked how much are the turtles. The store owner said 30 dollars. Layla was so excited then she remembered she didn't have any money, just like her mom didn't have enough money for her car.

They continued to look and finally she found the perfect turtle. The turtle had a beautiful colorful shell. She named him Manny. Her mom asked why she named him Manny and she told her its short for Manifesting. Manny the manifesting turtle. They laughed and left the store.

Every day after that, Layla would ask her parents to take her to the store to check on Manny.

Her parents worked hard. Her mom stayed late at work, and her dad planned their family vacation.

Chores list
- Laundry
- Dust
- Mop
- Sweep
- Garbage

First, Layla had a chores list she did the dishes, laundry, and cleaned up around the house in order to earn money.

Then, she went to the library to read books about turtles. Finally, she was able to go to the pet store. She was saving all the money that her parents gave her so she could buy Manny. Layla then realized she is going to need more than 30 dollars. She had to feed Manny, get him a tank, and toys.

AHA said Layla, I have an idea! A lemonade stand, she went to her backyard and began to pick lemons. She asked her dad to help her make lemonade. One by one her neighbors came and bought all of the lemonade.

At the end of the night, Layla asked her dad to help her count her money. While counting, her dad asked her where she wants to go on vacation. "Florida!" Layla said. Great idea, says Layla's dad, that is where we will go on vacation.

Three weeks later Layla finally had enough money to buy Manny but she didn't have enough money for the tank, food, or toys. After completing all of her chores, Layla and her dad drove to the pet store.

October

Mon	Tues	Wed	Thur	Fri	Sat	Sun
1	2	③	X 4	X 5	X 6	X 7
X 8	X 9	X 10	X 11	X 12	X 13	X 14
X 15	X 16	X 17	X 18	X 19	X 20	X 21
X 22	X 23	24	25	26	27	28
29	30	31				

Turtle Food

As, they were driving, her dad said, "your mom is at the car shop, she is buying the pink car she wanted!" Layla was so proud of her. She told herself, " if my mom can do it, I can do it too."

After getting to the store, Layla rushed to the turtle tank. To her surprise Manny was not there. Layla went to the pet store worker and asked, "did someone buy a turtle, I can't find my turtle." The worker said yes, a woman bought a turtle an hour ago.

Layla started crying. As they left the store she remembered that her mom told her she could do anything she set her mind to. As long as she believes she can do something, she will. She worked hard to make her dream of having a turtle come true, but it didn't work.

Layla's dad said "maybe it wasn't the right time". Layla mumbled, "it was the right time mom got her car, so I should have Manny." When Layla arrived home, she saw her mom's pink car parked outside.

Layla ran upstairs crying. Her mom followed her and asked, "What's wrong honey?" With tears in her eyes, she told her mom that somebody bought Manny. Her mom said, "everything will happen when it is supposed to happen." She wiped Layla's tears and told her to walk into her room.

To Layla's surprise she opened the door and there was Manny. Her mom bought her the food and the tank for her new pet turtle. Manny was swimming around and she was so excited. She ran and hugged her mom.

Completed Goals

Layla thanked her mom and told her she made her dreams come true. Her mom said, "no honey, you made your own dreams come true, I am so proud of you, you deserve it." At the end Layla got her turtle, her mom got her car and her dad got the vacation.

That day Layla's parents taught her a powerful message; Never underestimate the power of your mind. Whatever you dream you can achieve you just have to focus on it and tell yourself you can do it.

THE END

Now it's your turn
Draw what you are manifesting

Made in the USA
Middletown, DE
10 April 2023

28548124R00020